MW01205736

Adonai's Lamb

MESSIAH
The King

Before I begin, I must resolve an issue that you may have concerning the bible. Some have said that the New Testament is a Gentile book and only for Gentiles. There is no Gentile bible because all of the scriptures in the Tanakh are Jewish and all of the scriptures in the New Testament are Jewish so that both books are Jewish books. The writers of the New Testament had no New Testament with which to reference. The whole of the New Testament is a testimony to the life, work, and ministry of Messiah. The mysteries that have been concealed in Tanakh are revealed in the New Testament as they happened at the coming of Messiah. Let me add that the books are not only for Jews but through the Jewish people they are presented to the world that includes all gentiles. Salvation is through Messiah that is a Jew but His atoning work is for the entire world.

At age thirteen, I was full of fire concerning all that I thought that I knew about life. My best friend was Jewish and I was Christian, at least as Christian as I thought I should be at age thirteen. That eventually would fade into the wild lifestyle that I had come to practice through my teen years and into my twenties. Through the years, time had carried my zeal and my best friend into the almost forgotten regions of my memory, as I had filed them away into history. I am guilty of having neglected a truly valuable and meaningful friendship with someone that had a positive effect on my life. However, I never lost the desire to find the answers concerning the salvation of the Jewish people. When I was fifteen, a Baptist preacher came to the door and was invited inside. He was witnessing Jesus Christ to several of us and I asked him about Jewish people. The answer that I got was not what I wanted to hear, so I argued with him for what seemed like an hour. The argument got so heated, that he at one point threw his bible against the wall and it fell to the floor. I won't elaborate on the details of the confrontation, but the end result was that I was not convinced of his opinion and he left. I believe that Adonai had created something inside of me through this encounter that put a chip on my shoulder concerning this subject. Over the past twenty-five years, I have studied the bible in depth and became a bible teacher at my church, all the while remembering the chip on my shoulder. I have not been in contact with my friend all these years; however, he still holds a prominent place in my heart. If it were not for him, I would have had a different perspective in my studies and would have missed out on many unique treasures found in the word of Adonai. I have a love and respect for the Jewish people that I might not have had and my journey might have gone another way. I use the Complete Jewish Bible translation for scripture reference because it shows the Jewish way that Yeshua lived on the earth and that He is Jewish. My earnest goal is to present in a very meaningful way, the Messiah of Adonai's word, so that what was hidden may be made visible. The truth is here and it is wonderful to know how much God loves His people and His great sacrifice to save that which was lost.

The need for salvation

The very existence of sin is an enormous banner to the fact that the heart of man is in great disrepair. The heart is where our passions reside and are nurtured and we follow after those passions in life. Those passions can serve both good and evil, but when sin is involved we can absolutely fall.

Jer 17:9-10 CJB "The heart is more deceitful than anything else and mortally sick. Who can fathom it? (10) I, Adonai, search the heart; I test inner motivations; in order to give to everyone what his actions and conduct deserve."

King David was a man after Adonai's own heart and became a great king, but he also had that propensity for sin. His heart was drawn to follow after Adonai, but the sin kept him at a distance. How many of us have that same passion for Adonai as did David?

The sacrifice was a substitution for the offender so that one could find forgiveness to appease the conscience and bring reconciliation.

Lev 17:11 CJB For the life of a creature is in the blood, and I have given it to you on the altar to make atonement for yourselves; for it is the blood that makes atonement because of the life.'

The penalty for sin is death; we have all committed sin and according to the perfection that Adonai requires in Torah, there is no one that can live. We owe a debt of eternity; who can pay that and yet live? Adonai provided the sacrifice for the atonement; the innocent life destroyed for the guilty so that there is remission and reconciliation. That is the only way to defeat death because death is the penalty and because Adonai is just, the penalty has to be paid.

Psa 14:1-3 CJB [For the leader. By David:] Fools say in their hearts, "There is no God." They deal corruptly, their deeds are vile, not one does what is right. (2) From heaven Adonai observes humankind to see if anyone has understanding, if anyone seeks God. (3) But all turn aside, all alike are corrupt; no one does what is right, not a single one.

What man on this earth can attain absolute perfection so that he may live? Today there are no animal sacrifices, but rather there is the sacrifice of repentance and of prayer and service and there is no blood. How could Adonai redeem His people and how could He ever redeem the Gentile? Adonai shows that righteousness comes from the heart, and service, rather than religion must be the adherence:

Isa 1:11-18 CJB "Why are all those sacrifices offered to me?" asks Adonai. "I'm fed up with burnt offerings of rams and the fat of fattened animals! I get no pleasure from the blood of bulls, lambs and goats! (12) Yes, you come to appear in my presence; but who asked you to do this, to trample through my courtyards? (13) Stop bringing worthless grain offerings! They are like disgusting incense to me! Rosh-Hodesh, Shabbat, calling convocations—I can't stand evil together with your assemblies! (14) Everything in me hates your Rosh-Hodesh and your festivals; they are a burden to me—I'm tired of putting up with them! (15) "When you spread out your hands, I will hide my eyes from you; no matter how much you pray, I won't be listening; because your hands are covered with blood. (16) "Wash yourselves clean! Get your evil deeds out of my sight! Stop doing evil, (17) learn to do good! Seek justice, relieve the oppressed, defend orphans, plead for the widow. (18) "Come now," says Adonai, "let's talk this over together. Even if your sins are like scarlet, they will be white as snow; even if they are red as crimson, they will be like wool.

The heart of Adonai is in doing right and serving justice and loving others. Religious ceremonies can become sin when the heart is not right with Adonai and these actions just become a repetitive function of the flesh and meaningless.

Isa 29:13 CJB Then Adonai said: "Because these people approach me with empty words, and the honor they bestow on me is mere lip-service; while in fact they have distanced their hearts from me, and their 'fear of me' is just a mitzvah of human origin—

You may seek for the coming of Messiah in a man that has clout with the people and a military leader that can restore the kingdom. How do you believe that a kingdom on this earth can survive long without corruption from men's hearts causing trouble in the administration? As long as there is sin in the hearts of people, there will be trouble because evil has alluring power to draw a man away from righteousness. If you change the heart of a man, then you can change the world.

There was a man that was preparing the way for Messiah, His name was Yochanan and he was baptizing people to repentance and then he saw Him; Messiah coming toward him:

Joh 1:29-31 CJB The next day, Yochanan saw Yeshua coming toward him and said, "Look! God's lamb! The one who is taking away the sin of the world! (30) This is the man I was talking about when I said, 'After me is coming someone who has come to rank above me, because he existed before me.' (31) I myself did not know who he was, but the reason I came immersing with water was so that he might be made known to Isra'el."

This was the great purpose and this was why Yeshua was born as a man, that He might fulfill Torah and the requirement of death for all of us.

Allow me to present to you a chapter out of the book of Isaiah that you may not have seen. This is the fulfillment of the sacrifice of the blood and it is the innocent that is destroyed for the guilty. The heart of man must be united with Adonai in order to overcome evil, so Adonai has dealt with the sin problem in that He sent Messiah, not as a great military leader in this world, but as the atoning sacrifice for the remission of sins.

Isa 53:1-12 CJB Who believes our report? To whom is the arm of Adonai revealed? (2) For before him he grew up like a young plant, like a root out of dry ground. He was not well-

formed or especially handsome; we saw him, but his appearance did not attract us. (3) People despised and avoided him, a man of pains, well acquainted with illness. Like someone from whom people turn their faces, he was despised; we did not value him. (4) In fact, it was our diseases he bore, our pains from which he suffered; yet we regarded him as punished, stricken and afflicted by God. (5) But he was wounded because of our crimes, crushed because of our sins; the disciplining that makes us whole fell on him, and by his bruises [Or: and in fellowship with him] we are healed. (6) We all, like sheep, went astray; we turned, each one, to his own way; yet Adonai laid on him the guilt of all of us. (7) Though mistreated, he was submissive—he did not open his mouth. Like a lamb led to be slaughtered, like a sheep silent before its shearers, he did not open his mouth. (8) After forcible arrest and sentencing, he was taken away; and none of his generation protested his being cut off from the land of the living for the crimes of my people, who deserved the punishment themselves. (9) He was given a grave among the wicked; in his death he was with a rich man. Although he had done no violence and had said nothing deceptive, (10) yet it pleased Adonai to crush him with illness, to see if he would present himself as a guilt offering. If he does, he will *see his offspring; and he will prolong his days; and at his hand Adonai's desire will be accomplished. (11) After this ordeal, he will see satisfaction. "By his knowing [pain and sacrifice], my righteous servant makes many righteous; it is for their sins that he suffers. (12) Therefore I will assign him a share with the great, he will divide the spoil with the mighty, for having exposed himself to death and being counted among the sinners, while actually bearing the sin of many and interceding for the offenders."*

Messiah had become the eternal once and for all sacrifice that was substituted for you and I so that Adonai's justice was served. Sin has been dealt with and has been punished. This same Messiah after having been sacrificed for us will return in the future as that great king that will restore the kingdom; He did not remain in the grave.

Psa 16:8-11 CJB I always set Adonai before me; with him at my right hand, I can never be moved; (9) so my heart is glad, my glory rejoices, and my body too rests in safety; (10) for you will not abandon me to Sh'ol, you will not let your faithful one see the Abyss. (11) You make me know the path of life; in your presence is unbounded joy, in your right hand eternal delight.

Another prophecy that bears witness with

Isaiah 53 is Psalm 22 and yet another description of the heart of Adonai:

Psa 22:1-31 CJB [For the leader. Set to "Sunrise." A psalm of David:] My God! My God! Why have you abandoned me? Why so far from helping me, so far from my anguished cries? (2) My God, by day I call to you, but you don't answer; likewise at night, but I get no relief. (3) Nevertheless, you are holy, enthroned on the praises of Isra'el. (4) In you our ancestors put their trust; they trusted, and you rescued them. (5) They cried to you and escaped; they trusted in you and were not disappointed. (6) But I am a worm, not a man, scorned by everyone, despised by the people. (7) All who see me jeer at me; they sneer and shake their heads: (8) "He committed himself to Adonai, so let him rescue him! Let him set him free if he takes such delight in him!" (9) But you are the one who took me from the womb, you made me trust when I was on my mother's breasts. (10) Since my birth I've been thrown on you; you are my God from my mother's womb. (11) Don't stay far from me, for trouble is near; and there is no one to help. (12) Many bulls surround me, wild bulls of Bashan close in on me. (13) They open their mouths wide against me, like ravening, roaring lions. (14) I am poured out like water; all my bones are out of joint; my heart has become like wax—it melts inside me; (15) my mouth is as dry as a fragment of a pot, my tongue sticks to my palate; you lay me down in the dust of death. (16) Dogs are all around me, a pack of villains closes in on me like a lion [at] my hands and feet. [Or: "They pierced my hands and feet."] (17) I can count every one of my bones, while they gaze at me and gloat. (18) They divide my garments among themselves; for my clothing they throw dice. (19) But you, Adonai, don't stay far away! My strength, come quickly to help me! (20) Rescue me from the sword, my life from the power of the dogs. (21) Save me from the lion's mouth! You have answered me from the wild bulls' horns. (22) I will proclaim your name to my kinsmen; right there in the assembly I will praise you: (23) "You who fear Adonai, praise him! All descendants of Ya`akov, glorify him! All descendants of Isra'el, stand in awe of him! (24) For he has not despised or abhorred the poverty of the poor; he did not hide his face from him but listened to his cry." (25) Because of you I give praise in the great assembly; I will fulfill my vows in the sight of those who fear him. (26) The poor will eat and be satisfied; those who seek Adonai will praise him; Your hearts will enjoy life forever. (27) All the ends of the earth will remember and turn to Adonai; all the clans of the nations will worship in your presence. (28) For the *kingdom belongs to Adonai, and he rules the nations. (29) All who prosper on the earth will eat and worship; all who go down to the dust will kneel before him, including him who can't keep himself alive. (30) A descendant will serve him; the next generation will be told of Adonai. (31) They will come and proclaim his righteousness to a people yet unborn, that he is the one who did it.*

Yeshua; while hanging on a cross and upon His dying breath, referenced this very psalm:

Mat 27:45-46 CJB From noon until three o'clock in the afternoon, all the Land was covered with darkness. (46) At about three, Yeshua uttered a loud cry, "Eli! Eli! L'mah sh'vaktani? (My God! My God! Why have you deserted me?)"

For the sin of the world He did this so that He could change the heart of man to prepare a great kingdom that will be forever. The debt has been paid and man through Messiah can reunite with Adonai. Man can now be filled up by the Spirit of Adonai and truth will be his guide now and throughout eternity, if he will receive Him. The sacrifice has been made and death has been defeated in Messiah. This is how He writes His Torah in the hearts of His people.

Jer 31:32-33 CJB "For this is the covenant I will make with the house of Isra'el after those days," says Adonai: "I will put my Torah within them and write it on their hearts; I will be their God, and they will be my people. (33) No longer will any of them teach his fellow community member or his brother, 'Know Adonai'; for all will know me, from the least of them to the greatest; because I will forgive their wickednesses and remember their sins no more."

Yeshua answers how this happens in these verses:

Joh 15:26 CJB "When the Counselor comes, whom I will send you from the Father—the Spirit of Truth, who keeps going out from the Father—he will testify on my behalf.

When the Spirit of truth comes into a man, then he can begin to see Yeshua the Messiah in the scriptures. He will become visible to all that will receive Him and they will see as they had not been able to see before.

Isa 52:13-15 CJB "See how my servant will succeed! He will be raised up, exalted, highly honored! (14) Just as many were appalled at him, because he was so disfigured that he didn't even seem human and simply no longer looked like a man, (15) so now he will startle many nations; because of him, kings will be speechless. For they will see what they had not been told, they will ponder things they had never heard."

This is the mystery that has now been revealed, that Messiah would come to heal the heart of man and make it ready to see His glory.

Eze 11:19-20 CJB and I will give them unity of heart. "I will put a new spirit among you." I will remove from their bodies the hearts of stone and give them hearts of flesh; (20) so that they will live by my regulations, obey my rulings and act by them. Then they will be my people, and I will be their God.

There was a man named Sha'ul and he was a zealous man concerning his faith but was not yet given that Spirit so that he could see, but one day he was met by Yeshua:

Act 9:1-6 CJB Meanwhile, Sha'ul, still breathing murderous threats against the Lord's talmidim, went to the cohen hagadol (2) and asked him for letters to the synagogues in Dammesek, authorizing him to arrest any people he might find, whether men or women, who belonged to "the Way," and bring them back to Yerushalayim. (3) He was on the road and nearing Dammesek, when suddenly a light from heaven flashed all around him. (4) Falling to the ground, he heard a voice saying to him, "Sha'ul! Sha'ul! Why do you keep persecuting me?" (5) "Sir, who are you?" he asked. "I am Yeshua, and you are persecuting me. (6) But get up, and go into the city, and you will be told what you have to do."

Sha'ul had received that Spirit and from then on he began to show in his letters, what he was seeing in the scriptures. They are the word of Adonai and they are truth concerning all of us.

Rom 1:1-4 CJB From: Sha'ul, a slave of the Messiah Yeshua, an emissary because I was called and set apart for the Good News of God. (2) God promised this Good News in advance through his prophets in the Tanakh. (3) It concerns his Son—he is descended from David physically; (4) he was powerfully demonstrated to be Son of God spiritually, set apart by his having been resurrected from the dead; he is Yeshua the Messiah, our Lord.

We were dead in our sinful nature and without hope for eternity, but Adonai made a way for us to be revived to life again. Today that life flows from Adonai, through the blood of His only begotten Son Yeshua, that has taken away the sin of the world.

The descendant

In the beginning, there was a beguiling creature that had caused the first man and the first woman to disobey Adonai's command. After the incident, there was a meeting between Adonai and all of the offenders. In passing judgment, Adonai had spoken a curse over the creature called "nâchâsh" or the serpent, that had beguiled the woman.

Gen 3:14-15 CJB Adonai, God, said to the serpent, "Because you have done this, you are cursed more than all livestock and wild animals. You will crawl on your belly and eat dust as long as you live. (15) I will put animosity between you and the woman, and between your descendant and her descendant; he will bruise your head, and you will bruise his heel."

The word in this passage for descendant is the word " zera'" which means seed or progeny, so the implication is that there will be a continuation of the line of the non-human nâchâsh. Also, the bible normally speaks of the lineage coming from the man, but in this case, Adonai speaks of the seed of the woman. I believe that Adonai is addressing much more than the serpent and the woman.

As Adonai speaks about the descendant of the serpent, He addresses him in a strange manner. **he will bruise your head, and you will bruise his heel."** Adonai seems to be speaking to an entity that is inhabiting the serpent and that will be around much farther into the future. I believe that Adonai is addressing spiritual darkness as in a fallen angelic being. This being would be the Satan or the leader of a host of fallen angelic beings.

Eze 28:12-15 CJB "Human being, raise a lament for the king of Tzor, and tell him that Adonai Elohim says: 'You put the seal on perfection; you were full of wisdom and perfect in beauty; (13) you were in `Eden, the garden of God; covered with all kinds of precious stones—carnelians, topaz, diamonds, *beryl, onyx, jasper, sapphires, green feldspar, emeralds; your pendants and jewels were made of gold, prepared the day you were created. (14) You were a keruv, protecting a large region; I placed you on God's holy mountain. You walked back and forth among stones of fire. (15) You were perfect in your ways from the day you were created, until unrighteousness was found in you.*

This would have been the first angel that fell; there are others that have followed him in their rebellion against Adonai.

Gen 6:1-4 CJB In time, when men began to multiply on earth, and daughters were born to them, (2) the sons of God saw that the daughters of men were attractive; and they took wives for themselves, whomever they chose. (3) Adonai said, "My Spirit will not live in human beings forever, for they too are flesh; therefore their life span is to be 120 years." (4) The N'filim were on the earth in those days, and also afterwards, when the sons of God came in to the daughters of men, and they bore children to them; these were the ancient heroes, men of renown.

Now we see the descendants of this serpent in that there are creatures that were not created by Adonai, but were a perversion of creation set about by fallen angels. This is a spiritual battle between good and evil in the universe and the enemy is the spiritual darkness that came from these fallen angels and their offspring.

The descendant of the woman is to be the adversary to this host of dark entities that have invaded earth. The interesting thing about the words of Adonai concerning the woman is that He addresses the seed of the woman and not of the man. Adonai exists outside of the realm of time and space because He is the creator of both, so He has given the clues for the future so that we may seek Him and find the answers that will glorify Him. There is a peculiar passage in the book of Isaiah that speaks to this seed of the woman:

Isa 7:13-14 CJB Then [the prophet] said, "Listen here, house of David! Is trying people's patience such a small thing for you that you must try the patience of my God as well? (14) Therefore Adonai himself will give you people a sign: the young woman [Or: "the virgin."] will become pregnant, bear a son and name him `Immanu El [God is with us].

The key word in these scriptures is "sign" the translation has to be "virgin" or else it would not be much of a sign. Consider this; the father passes the blood to the child, not the mother, so in this way, the virgin has not procreated with fallen man but is endowed with divine seed from Adonai. The Son that she carries is infused with divine blood from Adonai hence "The Son of Adonai". This would be the reason to call Him Immanuel because He is "God with us".

Genesis 3:15 is a prophecy of the Messiah that would come in the future that would overcome sin and evil. Many books can and have been written about the descendant of this serpent. The descendant of the serpent is not of mankind but of a spiritual darkness that even today permeates societies with great deception. This book, however, is dedicated to enlightening the heart of the reader of the Messiah that has bruised the head of the descendant of this serpent.

To further add to this Immanuel that will be born to the virgin woman, we must investigate His name. Knowing that the New Testament is a Jewish book we should look there to find the name.

Mat 1:18-21 CJB Here is how the birth of Yeshua the Messiah took place. When his mother Miryam was engaged to Yosef, before they were married, she was found to be pregnant from the Ruach HaKodesh. (19) Her husband-to-be, Yosef, was a man who did what was right; so he made plans to break the engagement quietly, rather than put her to public shame. (20) But while he was thinking about this, an angel of Adonai appeared to him in a dream and said, "Yosef, son of David, do not be afraid to take Miryam home with you as your wife; for what has been conceived in her is from the Ruach HaKodesh. (21) She will give birth to a son, and you are to name

him Yeshua, [which means 'Adonai saves,']
because he will save his people from their
sins."

Many people call Him "Jesus" because the
Greek translation of Yeshua is Iēsous and this
transliterated into English is "Jesus". But
translated from Hebrew is "Joshua" which
actually means "God is salvation" or literally "
Jehovah-saved". There is no coincidence here
because Adonai has orchestrated the coming of
Messiah and has left nothing to be
misunderstood. If we consider the book of
Joshua, it is a book of the conquest to take the
promised land and this essentially is the
subject of salvation. Yeshua has invaded the
land of the enemy in the spirit realm and made
conquest for the promised salvation of His
people. In this subject, the whole world of
people is His mission, so that there are none
that are lost that receive the truth. We follow
Him in the conquest for the eternal souls of
humanity.

Joh 3:16-17 CJB "For God so loved the world
that he gave his only and unique Son, so that
everyone who trusts in him may have eternal
life, instead of being utterly destroyed. (17)
For God did not send the Son into the world to
judge the world, but rather so that through
him, the world might be saved.

He will return as the conquering King one day and take the kingdoms of the earth, but that is for another chapter. Now there is another issue that we must address concerning the prophecy of Genesis 3:15. The verse says; *"**he will bruise your head, and you will bruise his heel"**.* How is it that the serpent will bruise the heel of Messiah? Now that man has sinned and he knows good and evil; the propensity to sin is always present. There is no one that can save his own soul because there is no one that is without sin. The sacrificial system was implemented for the purpose of atonement, but that is only temporary. The imagery is that the blood is the atoning factor because, without the shedding of the blood, there is no remission. Remember that the blood comes from the father and not the mother, so the blood of the Son of Adonai is eternally symbolic of the atonement. The blood of Messiah was shed for the remission of sins, thus atoning forever, the souls that receive Him, so that we can enter eternity washed and clean. The bruising of His heel was the death of the sacrifice and He bore our sins and paid the cost in His own body thus was bruised by the hand of Satan.

Psa 136:26 CJB Give thanks to the God of heaven, for his grace continues forever.

Before the atoning work of Messiah, there was a fact that man as having been beguiled by the serpent, had given his authority over to evil, and the battle had begun. That is why the kingdoms of the world are corrupted. The souls and minds of people are in a condition of bondage to the sin nature and thus Satan has much influence to deceive them. The only way to escape that prison of deception is to know the truth and receive the truth.

Joh 8:31-36 CJB So Yeshua said to the Judeans who had trusted him, "If you obey what I say, then you are really my talmidim, (32) you will know the truth, and the truth will set you free." (33) They answered, "We are the seed of Avraham and have never been slaves to anyone; so what do you mean by saying, 'You will be set free'?" (34) Yeshua answered them, "Yes, indeed! I tell you that everyone who practices sin is a slave of sin. (35) Now a slave does not remain with a family forever, but a son does remain with it forever. (36) So if the Son frees you, you will really be free!

Isa 61:1-2 CJB The Spirit of Adonai Elohim is upon me, because Adonai has anointed me to announce good news to the poor. He has sent me to heal the brokenhearted; to proclaim freedom to the captives, to let out into light those bound in the dark; (2) to proclaim the year of the favor of Adonai and the day of vengeance of our God; to comfort all who mourn,...

Satan's power is death and his doctrines prove that out in our world, but when Messiah was raised from the dead, Satan's power was nullified. Everyone that comes to Messiah will live, so the only power Satan has left is his deception, thus his head is bruised.

Isa 9:1 CJB The people living in darkness have seen a great light; upon those living in the land that lies in the shadow of death, light has dawned.

Yeshua has set the captives free from the bondage of sin, so that we may refuse the deception of Satan and follow after Adonai as sons.

Adonai will provide

Gen 22:1-2 CJB After these things, God tested Avraham. He said to him, "Avraham!" and he answered, "Here I am." (2) He said, "Take your son, your only son, whom you love, Yitz'chak; and go to the land of Moriyah. There you are to offer him as a burnt offering on a mountain that I will point out to you."

Avraham had two sons, however, Adonai only recognized the son of the promise as a sacrifice in calling him his only son. This was the progeny that Adonai had promised to Avraham and now he was to offer him up, this son that was to become as many as the stars in the heavens in number. How can a man understand the ways of Adonai? He cannot fathom the purpose for all that Adonai does in the lives of His children. But Adonai had a great purpose for the way that He tested Avraham; Adonai was pleased with the faith of Avraham.

Gen 15:5-6 CJB Then the LORD took Abram outside and said, "Look at the sky and see if you can count the stars. That's how many descendants you will have." (6) Abram believed the LORD, and the LORD was pleased with him.

Avraham was told to go to the land of Moriah, and to a mountain that Adonai would show to him.

Gen 22:3-4 CJB Avraham got up early in the morning, saddled his donkey, and took two of his young men with him, together with Yitz'chak his son. He cut the wood for the burnt offering, departed and went toward the place God had told him about. (4) On the third day, Avraham raised his eyes and saw the place in the distance.

This place was a very special place that would hold enormous significance for the future. Even today it is a place of great controversy, not only for Israel but for the whole world. Avraham trusted in the absolute perfection of the will of Adonai so much so that he did not question this command.

Gen 22:6-8 CJB Avraham took the wood for the burnt offering and laid it on Yitz'chak his son. Then he took in his hand the fire and the knife, and they both went on together. (7) Yitz'chak spoke to Avraham his father: "My father?" He answered, "Here I am, my son." He said, "I see the fire and the wood, but where is the lamb for a burnt offering?" (8) Avraham replied, "God will provide himself the lamb for a burnt offering, my son"; and they both went on together.

Avraham the friend of Adonai prophesied of Messiah on this day as Adonai would one day provide the lamb for His sacrifice. Avraham prepared his son and raised his knife for to slay this most precious sacrifice by faith in obedience to Adonai. There must have been many tears mingled into this sacrifice that made it even more valuable to Adonai in that His faithful friend trusted Him so much. Even before he was to sacrifice his son, Avraham had already trusted Adonai with his son's life because he had done this in his broken heart already. This is the trust that Adonai seeks, in that we must trust Him with our very existence as much as Avraham trusted Him. Adonai will not ask you to sacrifice your son because the sacrifice has been made once and for all eternity. Avraham would not have to sacrifice his son that day but was halted by the Angel of Adonai.

Gen 22:11-13 CJB But the angel of Adonai called to him out of heaven: "Avraham? Avraham!" He answered, "Here I am." (12) He said, "Don't lay your hand on the boy! Don't do anything to him! For now I know that you are a man who fears God, because you have not withheld your son, your only son, from me." (13) Avraham raised his eyes and looked, and there behind him was a ram caught in the bushes by its horns. Avraham went and took the ram and offered it up as a burnt offering in place of his son.

There came a time when Adonai, in the same place where He commanded that Avraham offer his only son, would fulfill that prophecy that Avraham had spoken to Yitz'chak. Adonai would provide a Lamb for a sacrifice on that fateful day when Yeshua, Adonai's only begotten Son would become the Lamb of God that takes away the sin of the world.

Joh 1:29 CJB The next day, Yochanan saw Yeshua coming toward him and said, "Look! God's lamb! The one who is taking away the sin of the world!

I cannot imagine how that Adonai must have grieved for His only begotten Son on the day that He gave Him for sacrifice, and there was no substitute for Him because He is the substitute. This was the Lamb that Avraham had spoken about and now was the time that

Adonai would provide His Son for us all. He was without spot or blemish and was the only one that was worthy for the sacrifice.

The Bread of Life

Mic 5:1 CJB But you, Beit-Lechem near Efrat, so small among the clans of Y'hudah, out of you will come forth to me the future ruler of Isra'el, whose origins are far in the past, back in ancient times.

It is appropriate that Messiah should be born in the House of Bread as He is the Bread of Life. We were starved of life because of sin and the prison of darkness through the spiritual wickedness that permeates the high places. Adonai rules and His will is determined against all unrighteousness that defies Him. The very place of Messiah's birth testifies of His divine essence.

Luk 2:1-7 CJB Around this time, Emperor Augustus issued an order for a census to be taken throughout the Empire. (2) This registration, the first of its kind, took place when Quirinius was governing in Syria. (3) Everyone went to be registered, each to his own town. (4) So Yosef, because he was a descendant of David, went up from the town of Natzeret in the Galil to the town of David, called Beit-Lechem, in Y'hudah, (5) to be registered, with Miryam, to whom he was engaged, and who was pregnant. (6) While they were there, the time came for her to give birth; (7) and she gave birth to her first child, a son. She wrapped him in cloth and laid him down in a feeding trough, because there was no space for them in the living-quarters.

How perfect are Adonai's ways and His voice is heard throughout the universe? This is no coincidence that the child is laid in a feeding trough, as there was no room for them in the lodging places. This is Adonai's Lamb that will take away the sin of the world and is born in a stable where the sheep are kept. This lamb is the spotless unblemished lamb for the sacrifice. Born near the place where the shepherds watch their sheep and where Messiah would be revealed.

Mic 4:8 CJB You, tower of the flock, hill of the daughter of Tziyon, to you your former sovereignty will return, the royal power of the daughter of Yerushalayim.

The Tower of the flock (Eder) was a place where the shepherds would watch their sheep because they could see far off. This was a place south of Jerusalem in the area of Bethlehem. Targum Jonathan describes this as the place where Messiah will be revealed:

And Jakob proceeded and spread his tent beyond the tower of Eder, the place from whence, it is to be, the King Meshiha will be revealed at the end of the days. (Targum Jonathan on Gen. 35:21)

This Messiah, born in the House of Bread would become the Bread of Life for a lost and dying world.

Joh 6:33-35 CJB for God's bread is the one who comes down out of heaven and gives life to the world." (34) They said to him, "Sir, give us this bread from now on." (35) Yeshua answered, "I am the bread which is life! Whoever comes to me will never go hungry, and whoever trusts in me will never be thirsty.

This is the Bread of affliction that would be broken for the sins of the world:

Deu 16:3 CJB You are not to eat any hametz with it; for seven days you are to eat with it matzah, the bread of affliction; for you came out of the land of Egypt in haste. Thus you will remember the day you left the land of Egypt as long as you live.

The bondage of Egypt representing the bondage of sin is the reason for the bread of affliction that would be broken. Messiah would suffer affliction as the sacrifice of Adonai for the sin of the world and thus new life emerges from His sacrifice because His mercy endures forever, and He is the Bread of Life.

Joh 6:51 CJB I am the living bread that has come down from heaven; if anyone eats this bread, he will live forever. Furthermore, the bread that I will give is my own flesh; and I will give it for the life of the world."

Yeshua was born for the purpose of trading His life for humanity so that we can come now into the presence of Adonai. Yeshua will inherit the world and we are His inheritance because He has conquered death and will return when the time is fulfilled. He is the coming King that will rule the earth from Jerusalem.

The Passover

The children of Israel had been crying out for deliverance from the dark recesses of the bondage in Egypt. Adonai had heard their cries and out of a burning bush that was not consumed, He gave His instructions to Moses. Adonai shows His great power over the land in the form of plagues that would devastate the empire. But Pharaoh's heart was hardened and the last plague that would come through the land would be death. Death would visit every household that was not represented by blood. There must have been a tension in the land of Egypt on the night of the visitation when death would come to touch the families of the land. As the darkness fell and the midnight hour drew relentlessly nearer to its final destination, the heartbeat would quicken and the thoughts of the mind would rehearse every scenario of horrible possibility. Like the calm before the storm, the night air would be still and the song of the crickets would fade into a thick blanket of quiet uncertainty. The Israelites are safely hiding behind their blood-soaked doors, eating their Passover Seders in haste with the bitter herbs and unleavened bread. How the bitter herbs must have taken on a strange new meaning to them as they began to hear voices crying out in the distance. One by one each voice would be joined by another until the land of the Egyptians became filled with deep moans of sorrow and wailing. But in the land of Goshen where the faithful were fulfilling Adonai's commands, there was not a sound heard, not even as much as a dog barking. The heart-wrenching cries of the grieving families of Egypt would prove to be too much for Pharaoh and he would let the Israelite people go. With all of their herds and all of their families and all of their substance; Pharaoh would have the Israelites thrust from the land of Egypt.

The lamb was slain for the exodus of Adonai's people and the blood was the protective covering that stayed the death angel from their dwelling. A picture emerges from the scriptures in that the innocent lamb was the substance of their release and the blood was their protection. This is the picture of the ultimate work of Messiah, in that He is the sacrifice that was made for the great exodus from the bondage of the sin and darkness that has bound the soul of man for so long.

On the night of the Passover, Yeshua told His disciples to prepare the Passover Seder in the upper room and when they had eaten, Yeshua instituted a new covenant:

Luk 22:14-20 CJB When the time came, Yeshua and the emissaries reclined at the table, (15) and he said to them, "I have really wanted so much to celebrate this Seder with you before I die! (16) For I tell you, it is certain that I will not celebrate it again until it is given its full meaning in the Kingdom of God." (17) Then, taking a cup of wine, he made the b'rakhah and said, "Take this and share it among yourselves. (18) For I tell you that from now on, I will not drink the 'fruit of the vine' until the Kingdom of God comes." (19) Also, taking a piece of matzah, he made the b'rakhah, broke it, gave it to them and said, "This is my body, which is being given for you; do this in memory of me." (20) He did the same with the cup after the meal, saying, "This cup is the New Covenant, ratified by my blood, which is being poured out for you.

This is the cup of redemption, the third cup of

the four after the lighting of the candles that Yeshua will drink with His life and become our deliverance:

Exo 6:6-7 CJB "Therefore, say to the people of Isra'el: 'I am Adonai. I will free you from the forced labor of the Egyptians, rescue you from their oppression, and redeem you with an outstretched arm and with great judgments. (7) I will take you as my people, and I will be your God. Then you will know that I am Adonai your God, who freed you from the forced labor of the Egyptians.

The promise of Adonai will be fulfilled in Yeshua, as His blood is shed for the remission forever. He was God, but He was also a man and was obedient to the promise and will of Adonai:

Mat 26:42 CJB A second time he went off and prayed. "My Father, if this cup cannot pass away unless I drink it, let what you want be done."

This blood, when applied to the heart, which is the door to the soul, will stay the executioner and the believer will have everlasting life. One of the interesting pieces of this mosaic is the bones of the sacrifice:

Exo 12:46-47 CJB It is to be eaten in one house. You are not to take any of the meat outside the house, and you are not to break any of its bones. (47) The whole community of Isra'el is to keep it.

The custom of the crucifixion was this; in order to hasten death, the legs of the condemned were to be broken so that they couldn't raise themselves to breathe and would suffocate. The sun was going down and the bodies were to be buried before Shabbat began because it was the preparation, so the legs were broken except for one man:

Joh 19:32-36 CJB The soldiers came and broke the legs of the first man who had been put on a stake beside Yeshua, then the legs of the other one; (33) but when they got to Yeshua and saw that he was already dead, they didn't break his legs. (34) However, one of the soldiers stabbed his side with a spear, and at once blood and water flowed out. (35) The man who saw it has testified about it, and his testimony is true. And he knows that he tells the truth, so you too can trust. (36) For these things happened in order to fulfill this passage of the Tanakh: "Not one of his bones will be broken."

This definitely connects Yeshua with the Passover and He is that Lamb that was slain from the founding of the world. The blood of an ordinary lamb was not sufficient to take away the sins forever, so it had to be divine blood from Adonai.

The firstborn

This is Adonai's only begotten Son; His firstborn.   I can't help but see a correlation between this and the tenth and final plague in Egypt which set free the Israelites from the bondage of slavery.   The firstborn of every family would die on that terrible night when death would visit the household of unbelief. Of all the plagues that struck Egypt, this was the one that set the captives free. The wages of sin is death and Egypt represented sin, in that they held Adonai's people in bitter bondage, they were captive to sin. The entire world is captive to sin; the bitterness of slavery whose whip tears deep into the soul of mankind.   But Adonai would give the firstborn of His own house that the stubborn hand of sin would release its unmerciful grip from His people.

Joh 3:16 CJB "For God so loved the world that he gave his only and unique Son, so that everyone who trusts in him may have eternal life, instead of being utterly destroyed.

It is also interesting to me that after the tenth plague, Adonai's people were thrust out of Egypt; a picture of sin thrusting the captives out of its kingdom. Every person who comes to the Son of Adonai is rejected by the world and is thrust out from its ways. When sin loses its grip in your life and you no longer desire the sinful things that you once did because you are convicted in your heart, then sinful people begin to turn their backs on you. Misery loves company and when you aren't miserable anymore then misery wants nothing to do with you. When light enters a room the darkness goes away, they can't abide together. So here we have it; because of the plague of death which the firstborn of Adonai has suffered; the captives of sin are set free. And because of this freedom, Adonai's people are thrust out from the kingdom of darkness.

Joh 8:36 CJB So if the Son frees you, you will really be free!

Luk 4:18-19 "The Spirit of Adonai is upon me; therefore he has anointed me to announce Good News to the poor; he has sent me to proclaim freedom for the imprisoned and renewed sight for the blind, to release those who have been crushed, (19) to proclaim a year of the favor of Adonai."

Yeshua came to set the captives free.

Fire

Yeshua knew what would befall Him and He went willingly to the slaughter. As He was brought before His examiners He didn't speak a word in His own defense. They brought false witnesses against Him because there was no blemish in Him and when they accused Him of blasphemy because He said that He was the Son of Adonai; little did they know that He never lied.

Isa 53:7 CJB Though mistreated, he was submissive—he did not open his mouth. Like a lamb led to be slaughtered, like a sheep silent before its shearers, he did not open his mouth.

Adonai commanded Avraham long ago to offer as He said his only son *Yitz'chak* on an altar for a burnt sacrifice. But Adonai stopped him from offering *Yitz'chak* and showed him a ram caught in the bushes so Adonai provided for Avraham that day, but now He is offering His only begotten Son for a sacrifice for Avraham's sin and everyone that will believe in His sacrificial Lamb Yeshua. Adonai would pour out the fire of His indignation upon His own Son like the roasting with fire; this is Adonai's chastisement for sin.

Isa 53:4-5 CJB In fact, it was our diseases he bore, our pains from which he suffered; yet we regarded him as punished, stricken and afflicted by God. (5) But he was wounded because of our crimes, crushed because of our sins; the disciplining that makes us whole fell on him, and by his bruises [Or: and in fellowship with him] we are healed.

Yeshua would endure being beaten and humiliated and then scourged savagely and with His flesh falling from His body, torn and bleeding; He would be rejected by His own as He stood before them. Yeshua was totally alone on that day and who can imagine the immense pain and grief that He must have felt as strangers determined His fate, and all the time knowing that He was innocent. But He had to be innocent; He was that Lamb without spot or blemish, chosen for the sacrifice. He was to be burned up in the fiery chastisement of Adonai's wrath against sin. Our sins were laid upon His back and He became a curse for us so that Adonai could punish Him in our stead.

Gal 3:13 CJB The Messiah redeemed us from the curse pronounced in the Torah by becoming cursed on our behalf; for the Tanakh says, "Everyone who hangs from a stake comes under a curse."

The new covenant

Jer 31:30-33 CJB "Here, the days are coming,"
says Adonai, "when I will make a new
covenant with the house of Isra'el and with the
house of Y'hudah. (31) It will not be like the
covenant I made with their fathers on the day
I took them by their hand and brought them
out of the land of Egypt; because they, for
their part, violated my covenant, even though
I, for my part, was a husband to them," says
Adonai. (32) "For this is the covenant I will
make with the house of Isra'el after those
days," says Adonai: "I will put my Torah
within them and write it on their hearts; I will
be their God, and they will be my people. (33)
No longer will any of them teach his fellow

community member or his brother, 'Know Adonai'; for all will know me, from the least of them to the greatest; because I will forgive their wickednesses and remember their sins no more."

Little did the disciples know that they were part of the greatest plan of Adonai. On this night Adonai was revealing a mystery that has been written in the scriptures from long ago, in fact, this plan of Adonai was settled before the world began. This Passover Seder would be the institution of a new covenant. Not only would this be a new covenant with the House of Israel, but would include everyone that would trust in Yeshua; Jew and Gentile alike. This was a blood covenant and it would be in Yeshua's own blood. On this night at the Passover, Yeshua would symbolically offer the bread as His body, as He is the Bread of Life and it would be broken for us. Then He offered the wine which is His blood of the new covenant which is shed for us. Yeshua would present the ultimate sacrifice that night; Himself. He said to do these things in remembrance of Him and as often as we do them we remember His death until He comes. Remembering is very important to Adonai because remembering makes it a part of us. He instructed the Israelites to remember His word and the Torah.

Deu 11:18-20 CJB Therefore, you are to store up these words of mine in your heart and in all your being; tie them on your hand as a sign; put them at the front of a headband around your forehead; (19) teach them carefully to your children, talking about them when you sit at home, when you are traveling on the road, when you lie down and when you get up; (20) and write them on the door-frames of your house and on your gates—

Yeshua is the Word and this is a picture of remembering Him to make Him Lord of your life that you may have true life.

Joh 1:1 CJB In the beginning was the Word, and the Word was with God, and the Word was God.

The Book is written of Him and when we receive Him into our hearts we are applying His blood sacrifice to our lives and thus remission of sins as is written. On this Passover, Adonai would prepare His Lamb for the slaughter and with the roasting with the fire of Adonai's wrath against sin.

In modern times there are three pieces of Matzo that are put into a bag which has three sections called a Matzah Tash, the middle piece of bread is broken in two and one-half is then broken up and given to all of the people at the Seder. Then the other half is hidden and later the children will search for it and upon finding it they will break it into pieces and give to everyone again and this would be the last of the food eaten. There is a symbolic message in this for the Messianic Jew concerning Yeshua. The three pieces of bread represent the Father, the Son, and the Ruach Hakodesh. The second piece representing the Son "Yeshua" who is the Bread of Life is broken for all; this represents His death for the sins of all mankind. But the hidden piece of bread means that there is a mystery that has been hidden from the non-Messianic Jew and that is that Messiah would come a second time. This is the time when He will set up His physical kingdom on the earth, and the bread at the last of the meal would represent the partaking of the eternal kingdom where we will live with Him forever. This is the kingdom that the Jews looked for when Yeshua walked among them, but they had a very different idea of Messiah's purpose in their day. Now, however, we know that Adonai had to first change the heart of man before He could redeem him forever.

The work is finished

Even in His tremendous pain and suffering, Yeshua set the example for us in loving His enemies. The ringing of the hammer as blow by excruciating blow; it drove the huge nails into the flesh of a dying Savior, and He forgave them while they were yet murdering Him. Yeshua was bigger than hatred and He proved His true love for all of us as He willingly received in His body the death that was due us. There is a picture of this in the book of numbers in the bible.

Num 21:8-9 CJB and Adonai answered Moshe: "Make a poisonous snake and put it on a pole. When anyone who has been bitten sees it, he will live." (9) Moshe made a bronze snake and put it on the pole; if a snake had bitten someone, then, when he looked toward the bronze snake, he stayed alive.

Yeshua was made sin for us and became as the serpent of brass so that when He was lifted up on the cross, everyone that looks to Him will not die. Adonai gave us pictures so that when the time comes we can remember and understand.

Joh 3:10-15 CJB Yeshua answered him, "You hold the office of teacher in Isra'el, and you don't know this? (11) Yes, indeed! I tell you that what we speak about, we know; and what we give evidence of, we have seen; but you people don't accept our evidence! (12) If you people don't believe me when I tell you about the things of the world, how will you believe me when I tell you about the things of heaven? (13) No one has gone up into heaven; there is only the one who has come down from heaven, the Son of Man. (14) Just as Moshe lifted up the serpent in the desert, so must the Son of Man be lifted up; (15) so that everyone who trusts in him may have eternal life.

The Torah condemns us because we have broken it and the penalty for that is death. But Yeshua fulfilled the Torah; He kept it and never broke it so He was found worthy of life; He was a perfect sacrifice. No man can be found worthy of life because all of us have broken Adonai's Torah, but Yeshua who was perfect took our punishment and brought our sins down to the grave to fulfill the requirement of justice. As He was hanging between Heaven and earth and breathed His last He said; "it is finished" and the veil of the temple was torn from the top to the bottom. The veil was in place in the temple to separate the Holy of Holies where Adonai's presence resided from the rest of the temple, which separated His presence from man. But the veil was torn from the top down not from the bottom up; this indicates that it was Adonai who tore that veil.

Mat 27:50-51 CJB But Yeshua, again crying out in a loud voice, yielded up his spirit. (51) At that moment the parokhet in the Temple was ripped in two from top to bottom; and there was an earthquake, with rocks splitting apart.

Yeshua removed the veil of separation between Adonai and man because sin had been dealt with once and for all. Now we no longer have to be separated from Adonai's presence because through Yeshua we can gain access to the Father and go before His throne.

1Ti 2:5-6 CJB For God is one; and there is but one Mediator between God and humanity, Yeshua the Messiah, himself human, (6) who gave himself as a ransom on behalf of all, thus providing testimony to God's purpose at just the right time.

They took the lifeless bloody scared and battered body of Yeshua down from the cross and they placed Him in a rich man's grave that was nearby. The Governor had guards placed in front of the tomb at the request of the religious leaders so that no one could steal the body and say that He rose from the dead, so they sealed the tomb and began their vigil.

Luk 24:1-8 CJB but the next day, while it was still very early, they took the spices they had prepared, went to the tomb, (2) and found the stone rolled away from the tomb! (3) On entering, they discovered that the body of the Lord Yeshua was gone! (4) They were standing there, not knowing what to think about it, when suddenly two men in dazzlingly bright clothing stood next to them. (5) Terror-stricken, they bowed down with their faces to the ground. The two men said to them, "Why are you looking for the living among the dead? (6) He is not here; he has been raised. Remember how he told you while he was still in the Galil, (7) 'The Son of Man must be delivered into the hands of sinful men and be executed on a stake as a criminal, but on the third day be raised again'?" (8) Then they remembered his words;

Now Yeshua had taken our sins to the grave where He left them but He was raised from the dead defeating death hell and the grave. To all believers in Yeshua; death has no more claim because we have been bought with a great price and have been set free from the slavery to sin and the curse of the Torah. When you trust in Him and His work at the cross, you are like the Hebrews on the night of the Passover because you stand in obedience to Adonai. Yeshua's blood is applied to the doorposts of your heart and when Adonai looks on the blood, death must pass over and move on so your soul that once had sinned will not die because the sacrifice of the Lamb has been accepted.

1Co 15:55 CJB "Death, where is your victory? Death, where is your sting?"

Yeshua is our exodus from the bondage of sin and death that we may go forth into freedom and eternal life.

This is the gospel; that Yeshuah paid the penalty for us so that we might believe in Him and have eternal life.

Joh 3:16 CJB "For God so loved the world that he gave his only and unique Son, so that everyone who trusts in him may have eternal life, instead of being utterly destroyed.

Rom 10:8-11 CJB What, then, does it say? "The word is near you, in your mouth and in your heart."—that is, the word about trust which we proclaim, namely, (9) that if you acknowledge publicly with your mouth that Yeshua is Lord and trust in your heart that God raised him from the dead, you will be delivered. (10) For with the heart one goes on trusting and thus continues toward righteousness, while with the mouth one keeps on making public acknowledgement and thus continues toward deliverance. (11) For the passage quoted says that everyone who rests his trust on him will not be humiliated.

There is no longer a division between Jew and Gentile because Adonai is unity and He has united His creation into a new creation.

Eph 2:6-15 CJB That is, God raised us up with the Messiah Yeshua and seated us with him in heaven, (7) in order to exhibit in the ages to come how infinitely rich is his grace, how great is his kindness toward us who are united with the Messiah Yeshua. (8) For you have been delivered by grace through trusting, and even this is not your accomplishment but God's gift. (9) You were not delivered by your own actions; therefore no one should boast. (10) For we are of God's making, created in union with the Messiah Yeshua for a life of good actions already prepared by God for us to do. (11) Therefore, remember your former state: you Gentiles by birth—called the Uncircumcised by those who, merely because of an operation on their flesh, are called the Circumcised— (12) at that time had no Messiah. You were estranged from the national life of Isra'el. You were foreigners to the covenants embodying God's promise. You were in this world without hope and without

God. (13) But now, you who were once far off have been brought near through the shedding of the Messiah's blood. (14) For he himself is our shalom—he has made us both one and has broken down the m'chitzah which divided us (15) by destroying in his own body the enmity occasioned by the Torah, with its commands set forth in the form of ordinances. He did this in order to create in union with himself from the two groups a single new humanity and thus make shalom,

In Yeshua, we are all children of Adonai. The work has been done and now all that come to Him, He will save and will in no wise cast out. Have you known Him today? There is great hope for eternity, though we are guilty; He made us clean through His blood and we are made righteous in Him. Amen.

The answer

Just look at all of the terrible things that people do to one another and the way that they spend their time. I don't mean everybody, but as you take a Birdseye view, you can see the total unrest of a world that has no peace. Today lawlessness is rampant and there seems to be no justice. Violence is everywhere around the world and there are many victims that suffer because there is nowhere for them to turn. People all around the world are divided; countries are divided and people are all fighting for something different. There is no time when there is global peace; the clouds of war are always billowing somewhere in the world. What is the answer; should there be a world dictator that would enforce his own rule of law? That couldn't work because there will always be revolutions that would keep war raging and there would still be no peace. You can't take liberties away from people without an enormous backlash. Peace in any nation comes with a cost so war is always necessary. Every group of people has to stand against tyranny and despotism. As long as there is evil in men's hearts there can be no peace. Sin is the cancer that has brought humanity to the brink of total destruction. The effects of sin have proven that mankind cannot effectively govern himself without injustice. If left unchecked; mankind might eventually destroy his own existence. Adonai calls for justice, He says to take care of the fatherless and widows; He says to love your neighbor as yourself. He gave His Torah that we might know how peace can be attained; however, He knew that man would never conform because he gravitates towards the sinful ways. He promised a kingdom and He will keep His promise. Sin is the enemy to peace and any kingdom that consists of sinful mankind cannot stand long. What is the answer then? This is a spiritual battle that we fight on a daily basis. Sin is what separates us from Adonai and keeps us from knowing Him.

Gen 4:7 CJB If you are doing what is good, shouldn't you hold your head high? And if you don't do what is good, sin is crouching at the door—it wants you, but you can rule over it."

We must overcome pride and do what is right, but always there is that resistance, the sin that crouches at the door. If we allow sin to come in then it will rule and lead us to destruction. Pride keeps the door open for the sin to come in and rule, but Adonai calls for humility.

Isa 57:14-21 CJB Then he will say, "Keep building! Keep building! Clear the way! Remove everything blocking my people's path!" (15) For thus says the High, Exalted One who lives forever, whose name is Holy: "I live in the high and holy place but also with the broken and humble, in order to revive the spirit of the humble and revive the hearts of the broken ones. (16) For I will not fight them forever or always nurse my anger; otherwise their spirits would faint before me, the creatures I myself have made. (17) It was because of their flagrant greed that I was angry and struck them; I hid myself and was angry, but they continued on their own rebellious way. (18) I have seen their ways, and I will heal them; I will lead them and give comfort to them and to those who mourn for them— (19) I will create the right words: 'Shalom shalom to those far off and to those nearby!' says Adonai; 'I will heal them!' " (20) But the wicked are like the restless sea— unable to be still, its waters toss up mud and dirt. (21) There is no shalom, says my God, for the wicked.

Messiah has two appearances on this earth to fulfill Adonai's plan for the ages. First He was given as the unblemished Lamb for the sacrifice of everyone:

Joh 3:16-21 CJB "For God so loved the world that he gave his only and unique Son, so that everyone who trusts in him may have eternal life, instead of being utterly destroyed. (17) For God did not send the Son into the world to judge the world, but rather so that through him, the world might be saved. (18) Those who trust in him are not judged; those who do not trust have been judged already, in that they have not trusted in the one who is God's only and unique Son. (19) "Now this is the judgment: the light has come into the world, but people loved the darkness rather than the light. Why? Because their actions were wicked. (20) For everyone who does evil things hates the light and avoids it, so that his actions won't be exposed. (21) But everyone who does what is true comes to the light, so that all may see that his actions are accomplished through God."

We all were strangers to Adonai and were separated from Him by sin, but He sent His Son to pay the awful cost that He would purchase His people from the wages of sin which is death.

Rom 6:23 CJB For what one earns from sin is death; but eternal life is what one receives as a free gift from God, in union with the Messiah Yeshua, our Lord.

We not only are delivered from sin but are made to be children of the Most High. Adonai has made the way for the lost to find their way back home again.

Joh 1:12-14 CJB But to as many as did receive him, to those who put their trust in his person and power, he gave the right to become children of God, (13) not because of bloodline, physical impulse or human intention, but because of God. (14) The Word became a human being and lived with us, and we saw his Sh'khinah, the Sh'khinah of the Father's only Son, full of grace and truth.

This is not the end of His gift to us, but as children, He will come and dwell inside of us and bring that light to shine from us.

Joh 14:15-17 CJB "If you love me, you will keep my commands; (16) and I will ask the Father, and he will give you another comforting Counselor like me, the Spirit of Truth, to be with you forever. (17) The world cannot receive him, because it neither sees nor knows him. You know him, because he is staying with you and will be united with you.

Adonai will love people through you because He is in you and you are His vessel to honor

Him with love. This is the kind of vessel that He will use to convert the wicked to become broken and find the life in Him. He will live His power through His people and bring life to many and fill His kingdom with kindness and love. This is the way that He will fill His kingdom with righteous people and no wickedness will be found there. He will trust you to do His work in the earth and to steward all that He has.

Luk 19:11-27 CJB While they were listening to this, Yeshua went on to tell a parable, because he was near Yerushalayim, and the people supposed that the Kingdom of God was about to appear at any moment. (12) Therefore he said, "A nobleman went to a country far away to have himself crowned king and then return. (13) Calling ten of his servants, he gave them ten manim [a maneh is about three months' wages] and said to them, 'Do business with this while I'm away.' (14) But his countrymen hated him, and they sent a delegation after him to say, 'We don't want this man to rule over us.' (15) "However, he returned, having been made king, and sent for the servants to whom he had given the money, to find out what each one had earned in his business dealings. (16) The first one came in and said, 'Sir, your maneh has earned ten more manim.' (17) 'Excellent!' he said to him. 'You are a good servant. Because you have been trustworthy in a small matter, I am putting you in charge of ten towns.' (18) The second one came and said, 'Sir, your maneh has earned five more manim; (19) and to this one he said, 'You be in charge of five towns.' (20) "Then another one came and said, 'Sir, here is your maneh. I kept it hidden in a piece of cloth, (21) because I was afraid of you—you take out what you didn't put in, and you harvest what you didn't plant.' (22) To him the master said, 'You wicked servant! I will judge you by your own words! So you knew, did you, that I was a severe man, taking out what I didn't put in and harvesting what I didn't plant? (23) Then why didn't you put my money in the bank? Then, when I returned, I would have gotten it back with interest!' (24) To those standing by, he said, 'Take the maneh from him and give it to the one with ten manim.' (25) They said to him, 'Sir, he already has ten manim!' (26) But the master answered, 'I tell you, everyone who has something will be given more; but from anyone who has nothing, even what he does have will be taken away. (27) However, as for these enemies of mine who did not want me to be their king, bring them here and execute them in my presence!' "

We are His inheritance and when He comes to establish His earthly kingdom, He will fill it with His inheritance. He has gone away to a far country and will return and be the King over the earth and will receive all that His servants have gathered and will appoint His administration to those that have been faithful to do His will and convert the wicked. You are unique in that Adonai has put His essence into you and is trusting you, if you have trusted His Son and He is expecting you to share your uniqueness with the world. The one that kept to himself is that wicked servant and all that he has will be taken from him and given to him that has been faithful. Yeshua had come to the earth preaching that the kingdom of Adonai is at hand and that we must repent:

Mat 4:12-17 CJB When Yeshua heard that Yochanan had been put in prison, he returned to the Galil; (13) but he left Natzeret and came to live in K'far-Nachum, a lake shore town near the boundary between Z'vulun and Naftali. (14) This happened in order to fulfill what Yesha`yahu the prophet had said, (15) "Land of Z'vulun and land of Naftali, toward the lake, beyond the Yarden, Galil-of-the-Goyim— (16) the people living in darkness have seen a great light; upon those living in the region, in the shadow of death, light has dawned." (17) From that time on, Yeshua began proclaiming, "Turn from your sins to God, for the Kingdom of Heaven is near!"

For two thousand years, Yeshua has been gathering His subjects into that kingdom and will return a second time with His inheritance and rule this earth which is His. He came as a man in the flesh and so dominion as man is His over the earth and Adonai's words stand true. He sent His Son in the flesh as a man and legal heir to the earth, so that He could redeem it from the dominion of sin. He will come again in clouds and great glory to overthrow the governments of the world and establish Adonai's kingdom and rule from Jerusalem.

Psa 2:1-12 CJB Why are the nations in an uproar, the peoples grumbling in vain? (2) The earth's kings are taking positions, leaders conspiring together, against Adonai and his anointed. (3) They cry, "Let's break their fetters! Let's throw off their chains!" (4) He who sits in heaven laughs; Adonai looks at them in derision. (5) Then in his anger he rebukes them, terrifies them in his fury. (6) "I myself have installed my king on Tziyon, my holy mountain." (7) "I will proclaim the decree: Adonai said to me, 'You are my son; today I became your father. (8) Ask of me, and I will make the nations your inheritance; the whole wide world will be your possession. (9) You will break them with an iron rod, shatter them like a clay pot.' " (10) Therefore, kings, be wise; be warned, you judges of the earth. (11) Serve Adonai with fear; rejoice, but with trembling. (12) Kiss the son [or: Kiss purely], lest he be angry, and you perish along the way, when suddenly his anger blazes. How blessed are all who take refuge in him.

Yeshua will sit on the throne of His father David and rule the earth and His subjects will find peace and will judge the earth as He has ordained His own kings to rule in that day.

Rev 11:15-17 CJB The seventh angel sounded his shofar; and there were loud voices in heaven, saying, "The kingdom of the world has become the Kingdom of our Lord and his Messiah, and he will rule forever and ever!" (16) The twenty-four elders sitting on their thrones in God's presence fell on their faces and worshipped God, (17) saying, "We thank you, Adonai, God of heaven's armies, the One who is and was, that you have taken your power and have begun to rule.

Where will you be when that day comes; will you be with Him? Today you can know this King personally as He is not far from us because His kingdom is on this earth now in the hearts of His subjects. He will rule in your life now if you will allow Him into your heart. He is the essence of love and power and His desire is that no one should perish, but that all would come to repentance and be saved.

Time is short and the day is far spent; Yeshua is alive and well and He will be returning soon, shouldn't we be about the King's business? My desire is that you will prepare to meet Him and learn of all His attributes. There is much more to be found of Yeshua in the Tanakh but the book would be volumes and the purpose of this book is to light a fire inside you so that you will search the scriptures to reveal His essence and come to know Him. He has done His work for you and has given you the power to become an ambassador in this earth to represent Him and the Kingdom. Will you trust Him today? May Adonai bless you and enrich you by His continuing Spirit and reveal His majesty to you in your journey. Shalom.

Made in the USA
Columbia, SC
31 October 2017